The Wild Life of MONKEYS

By Camilla de la Bédoyère

WINDMILL BOOKS

THE WILD SIDE

Published in 2015 by **WINDMILL BOOKS**, an Imprint of Rosen Publishing
29 East 21st Street, New York, NY 10010

Publishing Director: Belinda Gallagher
Creative Director: Jo Cowan
Editorial Director: Rosie McGuire
Editor: Sarah Parkin
Designers: Jo Cowan, Joe Jones
Image Manager: Liberty Newton
Production Manager: Elizabeth Collins
Reprographics: Stephan Davis, Anthony Cambray, Jennifer Hunt

ACKNOWLEDGEMENTS

The publishers would like to thank Mike Foster (Maltings Partnership), Joe Jones, and Richard Watson (Bright Agency) for
the illustrations they contributed to this book. All other artwork from the Miles Kelly Artwork Bank.

The publishers would like to thank the following sources for the use of their photographs: t = top, b = bottom, l = left,
r = right, c = center, bg = background, rt = repeated throughout. **Cover** (front) Ingo Arndt/Minden Pictures/FLPA; (back)
worldswildlifewonders; (speech panel) Tropinina Olga. **Alamy** 6 dbimages. **FLPA** 1 Ingo Arndt/Minden Pictures; 4–5 Pete
Oxford/Minden Pictures; 7(tl) Ignacio Yufera; 11(t) Ignacio Yufera; 12 Pete Oxford/Minden Pictures; 13(tl) Neil Bowman, (r)
Edward Myles; 14–15 Piotr Naskrecki/Minden Pictures; 18 Ingo Arndt/Minden Pictures; 21(r) Paul Hobson. **Fotolia** Heading
panel(rt) Darren Hester. **Nature Picture Library** 15(br) Andy Rouse; 21(tl) Yukihiro Fukuda. **Photo Discs/ ImageState**
16–17(bg). **Shutterstock** Joke panel(rt) Tropinina Olga; Learn a Word panel(rt) donatas1205; 3 Worakit Sirijinda; 5(gorilla)
Mike Price, (orang-utan) javarman, (chimpanzee) Stephen Meese; 7(br) Mike Tan C. T.; 8–9(bg) andere; 8(tr) andere, (tl)
Jikinaargo, (fruits, also used on page 17) Andra Popovici, (paper, cl) happydancing, (frame, cl) Lisa Fischer, (cr) Anna Ts, (b)
jennipenni89, (banana split, b) Melissa Patton; 9(paper, t) House @ Brasil Art Studio, (tl) Noedelhap, (brush stroke, cl) Ambient
Ideas; 10 worldswildlifewonders; 11(b) redswept; 16(cr) Mariia Sats, (b) donatas1205; 17(paper, tl) sharpner, (tr) Jana Guothova,
(bl) jennipenni89, (cr) Lorelyn Medina; 19(tl) hallam creations, (b) Kjersti Joergensen; 20(b) Eric Gevaert.

LIBRARY OF CONGRESS CATALOGING-IN-PUBLICATION DATA

De la Bédoyère, Camilla, author.
 The wild life of monkeys / Camilla de la Bedoyere.
    pages cm. — (The wild side)
 Includes index.
 ISBN 978-1-4777-5511-2 (pbk.)
 ISBN 978-1-4777-5510-5 (6 pack)
 ISBN 978-1-4777-5512-9 (library binding)
 1. Monkeys—Juvenile literature. I. Title.
 QL737.P9D435 2015
 599.8—dc23

                    2014027101

Manufactured in the United States of America
CPSIA Compliance Information: Batch #CW15WM: For Further Information contact Rosen Publishing, New York, New York at 1-800-237-9932

Contents

What are you?

I am a monkey!

I am a type of animal called a primate. Primates are very clever and most have fur.

Furry body

Humans are primates too!

Long arms

Hands with fingers and thumbs

4

What is an ape?

Like monkeys, apes are primates. They are larger than monkeys and don't have tails.

Gorilla

Orangutan

Chimpanzee

Tail

5

What do you eat?

We eat lots of different things.

I pick juicy fruits off the trees, but I also like to eat bugs.

Fruit

Messy eater

Vervet monkeys eat nectar from flowers, but they get covered in yellow pollen too!

Flowers

Q. Why did the monkey go crazy?

A. Because all monkeys are bananas!

LEARN A WORD:
pollen
Yellow or orange powder found inside flowers.

Leaf lollipop

Thirsty monkeys lick water off leaves. They tear the leaves before eating them.

Leaves

Activity time

Get ready to make and do!

Banana split

YOU WILL NEED:
ice cream · banana
whipped cream
cherries

HERE'S HOW: Scoop the
ice cream into a dish.
Then slice the banana
into two long pieces.
Put the banana pieces
on either side of the
ice cream. Decorate
with whipped cream
and cherries. Enjoy!

Go ape!

Ask a grown-up to take
you to the park, where
you can practice your
monkey skills safely. You
will need to run, jump,
climb, and swing!

Ask for help!

8

Monkey face

Ask for help!

YOU WILL NEED:
paper plate · paints
paintbrush · paper
pencil · scissors · glue

HERE'S HOW:

1. Paint a paper
   plate brown,
   or glue brown
   paper onto it.

2. On separate paper, draw
   two eyes, a nose, a mouth,
   and two ears.

3. Cut them out, and
   glue them to
   the paper
   plate.

Now color me in and give me a name!

Draw a monkey

YOU WILL NEED: pencils · paper

1. Draw a squashed
   circle and two
   rounded shapes
   for ears.

2. Add another
   squashed circle
   at the bottom.

3. Draw the face
   and add two eyes
   and a mouth.

Where do you live?

I live in a rainforest, where there are lots of trees.

I can jump and swing from branch to branch. I use my tail to hang from trees.

Spider monkey

LEARN A WORD:

rainforest
Thick forest that grows in warm places where there is both sunshine and rain every day.

Ground life

Gelada baboons live in grassy areas where there are no trees. They sit on the ground and eat grass and roots.

Steam baths

Japanese macaques live on cold mountains in Japan. They sit in hot water pools to keep warm.

How smart are you?

We are very smart!

I use a stone to open the hard shell of a nut. Then I eat the nut inside.

LEARN A WORD:
intelligent
Animals that are intelligent are clever. They can learn new things.

Capuchin

Washing up

Macaque moms teach their young how to wash their food.

Q. How do you open a box of bananas?
A. Use a mon-key!

Clever chimps

Apes are intelligent, too. Chimps poke sticks into termite nests and use them to catch the tasty bugs.

Can you talk?

We can talk, but we don't use words.

We make lots of different sounds and make lots of different faces.

Q. Why don't monkeys play cards in the jungle?

A. Because there are too many cheetahs!

Howler monkeys whoop and .... bark to each other

15

Puzzle time

Can you solve all the puzzles?

Start here

Monkey maze

This monkey is so smart he found his way through the maze to find a banana. Are you as smart as him? Find your way to the middle of the maze.

Tell us apart

There are three differences between Mark and Matthew – can you spot them?

Mark

Matthew

Rhyme time

Only four of these words rhyme with "ape." Can you find them?

grape   mate   shape
scrape   bake   monkey
cape   chimp

Answer: grape shape scrape cape

True or False?

1. Monkeys and apes are primates.
2. Apes have tails.
3. Monkeys have hands with fingers and thumbs.

Answers: 1. True 2. False 3. True

Monkey puzzle

Mother monkey climbed a tree and picked four bananas. Father monkey picked two plums. Baby monkey picked one mango. Can you work out how may pieces of fruit the monkey family had picked altogether?

Answer: Seven

What color are you?

I am red, blue, gold, black, white, and brown!

I am the most colorful of all primates.

Q. What did the monkey wear to cook dinner?

A. An ape-ron!

Mandrill

Good-looking

The De Brazza's monkey has a long white beard and an orange patch of fur above its eyes.

Big nose

Male proboscis monkeys have orange fur. Their noses are so big that they wobble when they run and jump.

19

Can your baby climb trees?

No, he is too young to climb trees.

My baby stays with me all of the time. He uses his hands to grab hold of my fur. I feed him with milk.

Squirrel monkeys

Lesson time

Monkeys teach their babies how to find food. They look under leaves for bugs, nuts and seeds.

Japanese macaques

Q. Why did the baboon go to the park?
A. To play on the monkey bars!

Young gorillas

Remember . . .

Gorillas are apes, not monkeys. Apes and monkeys are two types of primates.

Playtime

Like young monkeys apes also love to play. They climb trees and chase each other.

Once upon a time, there was a man who earned his money by traveling around with a performing monkey. One evening the man came home looking sad and said, "The monkey is now too old to do his tricks. I will have to sell him to the zoo and make what money out of him I can."

The monkey heard this, and he decided to visit his friend the wild boar to ask him for help. The monkey sneaked out of the house and ran to the forest. He told the boar what his master had said. The boar said, "Does your master have a baby?"

"Yes," said the monkey, "he has one son."

"Does it lie near the porch in the morning? I will come around early and take the baby and run off with it. Then you must run after me and rescue the baby. When the zookeeper comes they won't want to sell you."

The monkey thanked the boar and went home. The next day, everything happened as the boar had planned. The mother placed the baby near the porch while she tidied the house. Suddenly there was a noise on the porch and a

cry from the baby. The mother called her husband, and they both ran to the porch door just in time to see the boar disappearing with their baby. Then they saw the monkey running after the thief.

The faithful monkey brought the baby safely back to their arms. "There!" said the wife. "This is the animal you want to sell to the zoo – if the monkey hadn't been here we would have lost our baby forever."

"You are right," said the man. "You may send the zookeeper back when he comes."

And when the zookeeper arrived, he was sent away. The monkey was well looked after and lived the rest of his days in peace and happiness.

Adapted from "The Sagacious Monkey and the Boar" by Yei Theodora Ozaki

Glossary

baboon a large monkey that lives on the ground and has a dog-like nose, and lives in groups

clever quick to understand and learn

macaque a medium-sized monkey that lives in the forest, and has a long face and cheek pouches for holding food

mango yellowish-red tropical fruit that is eaten ripe

primates the group of animals that includes human beings, apes, and monkeys

roots the parts of a plant that attach it to the ground

scrape to rub or push hard against a surface

split to break into two parts, usually along the middle

squash to press something so it becomes out of shape

termite a small insect that often feeds on wood

Index

Websites

For web resources related to the subject of this book, go to: **www.windmillbooks.com/weblinks** and select this book's title.